STEVE JOBS:

FROM APPLES TO APPS

EXTRAORDINARY SUCCESS WITH A HIGH SCHOOL DIPLOMA OR LESS

JENNIFER ANISTON: FROM FRIENDS TO FILMS

TYRA BANKS: FROM THE RUNWAY TO THE TELEVISION SCREEN

HALLE BERRY: FROM BEAUTY QUEEN TO OSCAR WINNER

JAMES CAMERON: FROM TRUCK DRIVER TO DIRECTOR

SIMON COWELL: FROM THE MAILROOM TO IDOL FAME

ELLEN DEGENERES: FROM COMEDY CLUB TO TALK SHOW

MICHAEL DELL: FROM CHILD ENTREPRENEUR TO COMPUTER MAGNATE

STEVE JOBS: FROM APPLES TO APPS

RACHAEL RAY: FROM CANDY COUNTER TO COOKING SHOW

RUSSELL SIMMONS: FROM THE STREETS TO THE MUSIC BUSINESS

JIM SKINNER: FROM BURGERS TO THE BOARDROOM

HARRY TRUMAN: FROM FARMER TO PRESIDENT

MARK ZUCKERBERG: FROM FACEBOOK TO FAMOUS

STEVE JOBS:

FROM APPLES TO APPS

by Jaime Seba

Mason Crest

STEVE JOBS: *FROM APPLES TO APPS*

Mason Crest
370 Reed Road
Broomall, Pennsylvania 19008
www.masoncrest.com

Printed and bound in the United States of America.

First printing
9 8 7 6 5 4 3 2 1

Library of Congress Cataloging-in-Publication Data

Seba, Jaime.
  Steve Jobs : from Apples to apps / Jaime Seba.
      p. cm. — (Extraordinary success with a high school diploma or less)
  Includes index.
  ISBN 978-1-4222-2299-7 (hardcover) — ISBN 978-1-4222-2293-5 (series hardcover)— ISBN 978-1-4222-9360-7 (ebook)
  1. Jobs, Steven, 1955- 2. Businesspeople—United States—Biography. 3. Apple Computer, Inc. 4. Computer industry—United States. 5. Computer engineers—United States—Biography. 6. Microcomputers—Biography. I. Title.
  HD9696.2.U62J638 2012
  338.7'61004092—dc23
  [B]
                              2011029218

Produced by Harding House Publishing Services, Inc.
www.hardinghousepages.com
Interior design by Camden Flath.
Cover design by Torque Advertising + Design.

CONTENTS

INTRODUCTION

Finding a great job without a college degree is hard to do—but it's possible. In fact, more and more, going to college doesn't necessarily guarantee you a job. In the past few years, only one in four college graduates find jobs in their field. And, according to the U.S. Bureau of Labor Statistics, eight out of the ten fastest-growing jobs don't require college degrees.

But that doesn't mean these jobs are easy to get. You'll need to be willing to work hard. And you'll also need something else. The people who build a successful career without college are all passionate about their work. They're excited about it. They're committed to getting better and better at what they do. They don't just want to make money. They want to make money doing something they truly love.

So a good place for you to start is to make a list of the things you find really interesting. What excites you? What do you love doing? Is there any way you could turn that into a job?

Now talk to people who already have jobs in that field. How did they get where they are today? Did they go to college—or did they find success through some other route? Do they know anyone else you can talk to? Talk to as many people as you can to get as many perspectives as possible.

According to the U.S. Department of Labor, two out of every three jobs require on-the-job training rather than a college degree. So your next step might be to find an entry-level position in the field that interests you. Don't expect to start at the top. Be willing to learn while you work your way up from the bottom.

That's what almost all the individuals in this series of books did: they started out somewhere that probably seemed pretty distant from their end goal—but it was actually the first step in their journey. Celebrity Simon Cowell began his career working in a mailroom. Jim Skinner, who ended up running McDonald's Corporation, started out flipping burgers. World-famous cook Rachael Ray worked at a candy counter. All these people found incredible success without a college degree—but they all had a dream of where they wanted to go in life . . . and they were willing to work hard to make their dream real.

Ask yourself: Do I have a dream? Am I willing to work hard to make it come true? The answers to those questions are important!

CHAPTER 1
EARLY LIFE

Words to Know

tablet computer: A tablet computer is a small computer that is mostly just a screen. Often, tablet computers have touch screen controls.

innovative: If something is innovative, it is a new idea or a new take on an existing idea.

CEO: CEO stands for chief executive officer. The CEO is responsible for making big decisions at a company.

benchmark: A benchmark is a standard or point of reference against which things are commonly compared.

On January 27, 2010, Steve Jobs introduced the world to the next big thing from Apple, the company Steve had helped found and make successful. The company had already released the iPod and iPhone, as well as countless versions of their Macintosh computer (also known as the Mac). With the iPod and iTunes, Apple changed the way people listened to music and bought the latest releases from their favorite artists. With the iPhone, Apple changed what people expected from a cell phone. With their latest creation,

Apple wanted to change the way people thought about computers. Standing on the stage at the Yerba Buena Center for the Arts in San Francisco, California, Steve announced that Apple would be releasing its first **tablet computer**, the iPad.

The iPad shared many characteristics with the much smaller iPhone. The new device had touch screen controls, could download apps, and allowed users to watch movies and listen to music. The iPad was much larger than the iPhone, though, designed to be a computer you can use on your couch while watching TV, not something you put in your pocket. Apple's move into tablet computers had been rumored for years, but in January 2010, Steve confirmed that the iPad would be available for purchase in the spring of the same year.

In April 2010, the iPad went on sale in the United States. In the first day that the iPad was available, Apple sold more than 300,000, and by the end of the first month, the company had sold more than a million. The iPad was another huge hit for Apple, just as the iPod and iPhone had been before it.

Apple unveiled its first home computer, the Macintosh, in 1984. Almost thirty years later, at the end of his life, Steve Jobs was still at the center of the company he helped start. But in October of 2011, the world was saddened to learn of Jobs' death. The world had lost one of the brightest minds of modern times. Under Jobs, Apple created products that were both popular and **innovative**. Since the Macintosh, Apple has become one of the most popular technology companies in the world. Before his death, Steve Jobs was one of the most famous **CEO**s of all time. Few people have

Steve Jobs introduces the iPad on January 27, 2010.

helped shape the direction of technology in the twenty-first century as much as Steve Jobs did.

The College Choice

There are few people who become as successful as Steve Jobs was—and even fewer successful individuals who have achieved so much success without a college degree. But Steve Jobs never graduated from college. He accomplished all that he did without ever achieving that **benchmark** of success.

In the last few decades, more and more high school graduates are going on to pursue college degrees. In 2009, 70 percent of all graduating high school seniors went on to college the

Today, Apple's headquarters is located in Cupertino, California, a long way from the garage where Steve Jobs started the company!

following year. For many young adults in high school, college seems like the obvious next step. After all, it's impossible to become a scientist, lawyer, doctor, or teacher without a college degree. But attending college is still a choice, and it's not for everyone. For some, achieving success doesn't require college. Many young people are driven to pursue their dreams without a college education. Some of them know exactly what they want to do for a living, and they know how to get where they want to go without having a college degree. Entering the workforce instead of attending college helps them learn new skills, make money, and gain work experience.

Steve Jobs attended college for a little while, but he never graduated with a degree. Instead, he went after a career in technology, eventually beginning his own company. Steve was driven to succeed and driven to learn about things he didn't understand. Steve became such a huge success because of that drive to reach his goals.

Steve's Early Life

Steve Jobs was born in San Francisco on February 24, 1955. His biological parents were college graduate students who put him up for adoption when he was born. In 2005, Steve talked about his biological mother and who she wanted to adopt him.

My biological mother was a young, unwed college graduate student, and she decided to put me up for adoption. She felt very strongly that I should be adopted by college graduates, so everything was all set for me to be adopted at birth by a lawyer and his wife. Except that when I popped out they decided at the last minute that they really wanted a girl. So my parents, who were on a waiting list, got a call in the middle of the night asking, "We have an unexpected baby boy; do you want him?" They said, "Of course."

But Steve's biological mother was disappointed to learn that his new mother had never finished college, and his new father had never graduated from high school. Determined that her son would experience higher education, Steve's birth mother had second thoughts about the adoption.

"She refused to sign the final adoption papers," he said. "She only relented a few months later when my parents promised that I would someday go to college."

Paul and Clara Jobs of Mountain View, Santa Clara County, California, finally adopted Steve. Paul was a machinist, and Clara was an accountant. They raised Steve and saved money so they could one day send him to college, fulfilling their promise to their son's birth mother. In 1958, Steve got a little sister when his parents Paul and Clara adopted a baby girl named Patti.

Steve was a smart child, but he also had a hard time giving school his full attention. In the fourth grade, a teacher named Mrs. Hill found that she had to pay Steve to get the gifted but distracted student to focus in an advanced class. She gave Steve five-dollar bills and candy in order to get him to complete schoolwork and pay attention to class. Steve ended up doing so well in Mrs. Hill's

Steve Jobs learned about computers by listening to lectures at Hewlett-Packard's headquarters in Palo Alto, California.

class that he skipped fifth grade and moved into middle school. He attended Crittenden Middle School for a little while, before moving with his family to Los Altos, where he began attending Cupertino Junior High School.

As a student at Cupertino Junior High School and later at Homestead High School in Cupertino, Steve continued to show his intelligence, but he still had trouble focusing on school. Interested in computers and technology, he grew up learning from the engineers in his town; he also frequently attended after-school lectures at the Hewlett-Packard Company in Palo Alto, California. But Steve was also often in trouble for misbehaving; some of his pranks included releasing snakes in a classroom.

In 1972, Steve graduated from high school and prepared himself to move on to college. His parents were keeping their promise to Steve's biological mother by making sure he continued his education after high school.

Steve at College

Steve enrolled in Reed College, a liberal arts school in Portland, Oregon. He didn't last long in the traditional college structure, however, and he soon left. In fact, he dropped out after just one semester.

"I never graduated from college. Truth be told, this is the closest I've ever gotten to a college graduation," Steve said, speaking to graduating students during a commencement address at Stanford University in 2005.

Steve went to Reed College in Oregon for a short time before starting his career with Apple.

I dropped out of Reed College after the first six months, but then stayed around as a drop-in for another eighteen months or so before I really quit. I naively chose a college that was almost as expensive as Stanford, and all of my working-class parents' savings were being spent on my college tuition. After six months, I couldn't see the value in it. I had no idea what I wanted to do with my life and no idea how college was going to help me figure it out. And here I was spending all of the money my parents had saved their entire life. So I decided to drop out and trust that it would all work out okay. It was pretty scary at the time, but looking back it was one of the best decisions I ever made. The minute I dropped out, I could stop taking the required classes that didn't interest me, and begin dropping in on the ones that looked interesting.

Once he was free from the rigid structure of required courses, Steve began to really enjoy being a student. Now he could take classes that interested him, regardless of whether they fell into a specific degree program. Still, despite being happy with his decision, that period in his life came with some struggles.

"It wasn't all romantic," Steve told Stanford's class of 2005.

I didn't have a dorm room, so I slept on the floor in friends' rooms. I returned Coke bottles for the five-cent deposits to buy food with, and I would walk the seven miles across town every Sunday night to get one good meal a week at the Hare Krishna temple. I loved it. And much of what I stumbled into by following my curiosity and intuition turned out to be price-less later on.

One of the classes Steve most enjoyed was calligraphy, a highly decorative style of writing. The Reed College campus was covered with examples of the beautiful type of art, from posters to labels. Steve was fascinated by the creativity and decided to join the class to learn how to do it himself.

"I learned about serif and san-serif typefaces, about varying the amount of space between different letter combinations, about what makes great typography great," Steve told the graduating students of Stanford. "It was beautiful, historical, artistically subtle in a way that science can't capture, and I found it fascinating. None of this had even a hope of any practical application in my life."

Or so he thought. A decade later, when Steve and his friends were busily working to design the first Macintosh computer, he recalled this uncommon skill he'd picked up during his short time in college.

"We designed it all into the Mac. It was the first computer with beautiful typography," said Jobs.

If I had never dropped in on that single course in college, the Mac would have never had multiple typefaces or proportion-ally spaced fonts. And since Windows just copied the Mac, it's likely that no personal computer would have them. If I had never dropped out, I would have never dropped in on this calligraphy class, and personal computers might not have the

A class on calligraphy had a huge influence on Steve Jobs' work on the first Macintosh computer.

wonderful typography that they do. Of course it was impossible to connect the dots looking forward when I was in college. But it was very, very clear looking backwards ten years later.

Although he didn't know it at the time, that calligraphy class gave Steve one of the skills that would help propel him to an elite status as one of the world's most innovative and creative minds of all time. "You can't connect the dots looking forward; you can only connect them looking backwards," he told the graduating class at Stanford. "So you have to trust that the dots will somehow connect in your future. You have to trust in something—your gut, destiny, life, karma, whatever. This approach has never let me down, and it has made all the difference in my life."

After College

In 1974, after leaving Reed College, Steve got a job working at Atari, one of the very first video game companies. Steve helped to create some of the era's most popular games while he worked at the company.

During this time, Steve was enthralled by the '70s' free-spirited atmosphere that was marked by the artistic brilliance of music legend Bob Dylan. "We'd drive huge distances to meet people who had . . . pictures or interviews with Bob Dylan," said Steve's good friend Steve Wozniak.

Steve met Wozniak when he was still in high school and the two remained friends through Steve's time at Reed College. Wozniak, known as "Woz," later went on to co-found Apple with Steve.

Steve was adventurous, and he wanted to see new things. He joined his friend, and future Apple employee, Daniel Kottke, on a backpacking trip to India and came back with a shaved head and a new perspective on life.

When Steve returned from India, he went back to his job at Atari, but soon he would be moving on to starting his own company with friend Steve Wozniak.

During his 2005 commencement address to students at Stanford University, Steve reminisced about a publication from his youth called *The Whole Earth Catalog*, which he called "one of the bibles of my generation."

"This was . . . before personal computers and desktop publishing, so it was all made with typewriters, scissors, and Polaroid cameras," Steve told the students at Stanford. "It was sort of like Google in paperback form, thirty-five years before Google came along: it was idealistic, and overflowing with neat tools and great notions."

When the final issue was published, the back cover included a photograph of a country road in the early morning. Beneath it were words that stayed seared in Steve's mind forever: "Stay hungry. Stay foolish."

"It was their farewell message as they signed off. Stay Hungry. Stay Foolish," he said to the Stanford students. "And I have always wished that for myself."

Those words summarize Steve's mindset as he began building a company that would play a major part in the technology revolution of the late twentieth century. He probably never dreamed that as result, he would one day become a household name.

CHAPTER 2
RISE TO SUCCESS

Words to Know

amplification: The process of making something larger, of expanding it, can be referred to as amplification.

eclectic: Something that's eclectic represents a broad range of tastes, styles, and ideas.

humanistic: The philosophy that human dignity is important and that humans will be able to solve their problems through science and reason is sometimes referred to as humanistic.

arcane: Something that is arcane is very mysterious; it can only be understood by a few people.

software: The programs that a computer runs are called software.

investors: Investors give a company money to make products or hire employees. Investors expect to make their money back if the company is successful.

producer: In movies, a producer helps to get the movie made by ensuring that every part of the film's creation goes smoothly and everyone working on the film has what's needed.

interim: Interim means in between or temporary.

patents: Patents are grants made by a government that confer upon the creator of an invention the sole right to make, use, and sell that invention for a set period of time.

democratize: To democratize is to make so everyone has access to it.

For Steve, finding his passion in life was his priority—and part of that meant working with his friends. He worked at Atari with his friend Steve Wozniak, designing video games. Woz was the stronger engineer, but Steve had creativity and business sense. The two designed and worked with computers as a hobby, becoming part of a group called the Homebrew Computer Club. Together, in 1976, they decided to create a new kind of computer, as well as a company focused on selling them.

Starting Apple

Before they could begin, however, the pair needed money. Steve sold his Volkswagen microbus, and Woz sold his prized Hewlett-Packard scientific calculator. With enough money to start their new company, the two began working in the Jobs family garage, slowly beginning to build what would become an empire.

"I was lucky—I found what I loved to do early in life," Steve said. "Woz and I started Apple in my parents' garage when I was twenty. We worked hard, and in ten years Apple had grown from just the two of us in a garage into a $2 billion company with over 4,000 employees."

The pair's first big sale, an order of fifty computers from a local electronics store, was the official start of the Apple Corporation. Steve reflected on these beginnings of Apple in his 2005 Stanford commencement address:

Apple was this incredible journey. I mean we did some amazing things there. The thing that bound us together at Apple was the

Steve founded Apple with his friend Steve Wozniak.

ability to make things that were going to change the world. That was very important. We were all pretty young. The average age in the company was mid-to-late twenties. Hardly anybody had families at the beginning and we all worked like maniacs and the greatest joy was that we felt we were fashioning collective works of art much like twentieth-century physics. Something important that would last, that people contributed to and then could give to more people; the **amplification** factor was very large.

Apple's first employee was Steve's friend Daniel Kottke, who had joined Steve on his trip to India. He was part of an **eclectic**

Macintosh computers allowed more people to use machines that were once too complicated for non-experts. Apple brought computers into the home more than ever before.

mix of young, creative innovators. All of the men involved in Apple's beginning, including Steve, were experienced in the use and creation of computers, but they also brought other passions to their work.

"The Macintosh turned out so well because the people working on it were musicians, artists, poets, and historians who also happened to be excellent computer scientists," Steve said.

As the company continued to grow, Apple was soon on the forefront of innovation. By making computers smaller and more user friendly, Apple paved the way for technologies and trends that have become so commonplace, most people can't imagine life without them. Steve—and Apple as a whole—focused on creating technically sound products, while at the same time always making computers as easy to use as possible.

"The things I'm most proud about at Apple is where the technical and the *humanistic* came together," Steve said.

The Macintosh basically revolutionized publishing and printing. The typographic artistry coupled with the technical understanding and excellence to implement that electronically—those two things came together and empowered people to use the computer without having to understand *arcane* computer commands. It was the combination of those two things that I'm the most proud of.

Although Apple was always pushing things forward and growing because of its innovative products, Steve also said that Apple's rise to success was partly due to luck. He called

Apple's early achievements a case of being "at the right place at the right time."

Whether by luck, innovation, or the intelligence of its founders, Apple also succeeded in creating a way of doing business that has been copied by other companies. Most modern computer and software companies that have achieved success have done so by copying the model created by Apple. Steve said:

> In doing the Macintosh, for example, there was a core group of less than a hundred people, and yet Apple shipped over ten million of them. Of course everybody's copied it and it's hundreds of millions now. That's pretty large amplification, a million to one. It's not often in your life that you get that opportunity to amplify your values a hundred to one, let alone a million to one. That's really what we were doing.

Apple was making more money than any of the founders could have imagined. Steve was worth $200 million by the time he was twenty-five, and he was on the cover of *Time* magazine the following year. The cover read, "Striking it rich, America's risk takers." Steve, with shaggy hair, mustache, and an apple on his head, was pictured next to an Apple computer.

But despite his important role in the creation and success of Apple, eventually Steve wasn't a good fit for the direction that Apple was heading. In 1985, he was fired from the company he had founded, and he decided it was time to move on.

Apple's logo and slogan "Think Different" became icons of the technology world as the company brought computers to the average consumer.

"I've been thinking a lot and it's time for me to get on with my life," he said at an Apple board meeting. "It's obvious that I've got to do something. I'm thirty years old."

The stunning change was the result of internal turmoil that had been going on at Apple for years.

"How can you get fired from a company you started?" he said, asking the question so many others were pondering at the time.

Well, as Apple grew we hired someone who I thought was very talented to run the company with me, and for the first year or so things went well. But then our visions of the future began to diverge and eventually we had a falling out. When we did, our Board of Directors sided with him. So at thirty I was out. And very publicly out. What had been the focus of my entire adult life was gone, and it was devastating.

What is Silicon Valley?

Silicon Valley is an area of California near San Francisco in which many of the country's technology companies are based or have started. Silicon Valley is often thought of as the center of the technology, Internet, and computer industries in the United States and even the world.

Steve Jobs, and many of Apple's early employees, grew up in or around the Silicon Valley. The beginnings of the American computer technology industry were all around the people who began Apple. And eventually, Apple would be one of the Valley's most well known companies.

The name "Silicon Valley" was first used in 1971, when the name appeared in a magazine article called "Silicon Valley in the USA." The "valley" is the Santa Clara Valley near San Francisco. Silicon is a material used in computer parts. Apple, Intel, Twitter, EBay, Yahoo!, and many other technology companies have been based in Silicon Valley at some point, and some of the biggest companies in the world were founded in the area. Stanford University is also in the Silicon Valley area.

When he left the company to which he'd devoted so much of himself to, Steve felt lost. And once again, he thought about what he wanted his life to be, and what he'd done so far.

"I really didn't know what to do for a few months," he said.

I felt that I had let the previous generation of entrepreneurs down—that I had dropped the baton as it was being passed to me. . . . I was a very public failure, and I even thought about running away from the [Silicon] Valley. But something slowly began to dawn on me—I still loved what I did. The turn of events at Apple had not changed that one bit. I had been rejected, but I was still in love. And so I decided to start over.

New Opportunities

Though Steve initially felt lost after leaving Apple, he was also able to do a variety of new things, both in business and personally. President Reagan awarded the National Technology Medal to Steve in 1985 and the Jefferson Award for Public Service in 1987. Two years later, Steve was named Entrepreneur of the Decade by *Inc.* magazine. Around the same time, Steve also fell in love with the woman who would become his wife, Laurene Powell. In March of 1991, the couple married, and that September, their first son, Reed, was born.

"I didn't see it then, but it turned out that getting fired from Apple was the best thing that could have ever happened to me," Steve said later. "The heaviness of being successful was replaced by the lightness of being a beginner again, less sure about everything. It freed me to enter one of the most creative periods of my life."

Steve also founded a new company called NeXt, which he attempted to build into a competitor for Apple. The company was focused on *software* at first, but soon moved into making computers. Steve served as the company's CEO, and Texas businessman Ross Perot was one of NeXt's major *investors*. Steve continued to run NeXt as he took a chance on a different kind of business.

Pixar

In 1986, Steve went in a new direction when he purchased a computer special-effects company called the Graphics Group from filmmaker George Lucas. The group had worked with Lucas's company, Lucasfilm, to help create special effects for years before Steve bought the company for five million dollars from the *Star Wars* creator. The company became independent and changed its name to Pixar Animation Studio. Steve became the CEO of the company.

In its early days, Pixar created a computer called the Pixar Image Computer, used by doctors and some parts of the government. Disney was interested in the computer for the way it could be used in animation. Due to poor sales of the computer, Pixar began working on advertisements, for candy, mouthwash, and other products. Soon, Pixar stopped making computers altogether, instead focusing on computer animation. Disney, aware of Pixar from its days as a computer company, saw the potential for computer-animated films targeted at kids and began working with Pixar to create a new kind of movie.

Walt Disney Pictures released *Toy Story*, the studio's first feature film, in 1995, and it was the highest-grossing film that year (in other words, it made the most money). Not only that, but the movie was also the third highest-grossing animated film of all time, and the first animated movie created entirely on a computer. Steve was a **producer** on the film.

Today, Pixar is known for beloved movies like *A Bug's Life*, *Monsters, Inc.*, *Finding Nemo*, *The Incredibles*, *Cars*, and *Ratatouille*. In 2006, after Pixar's merger with the Walt Disney Company, Steve went on to serve on Disney's board of directors.

Returning to Apple

When Steve began NeXt in 1985, he intended to build a company that could compete with Apple, but it didn't work out that way. Instead, NeXt Software was sold to Apple in 1996,

Pixar Place at Disney's Hollywood studios is just one example of how big Pixar has become since Steve Jobs helped to start the company.

and the following year, Steve returned to Apple as *interim* CEO and chairman.

Over the next fifteen years, Jobs was involved in the day-to-day operations of Apple. He was in charge of every aspect of the company, from the development of the wildly popular iPod to the choice of chef in the cafeteria. He was the self-proclaimed co-inventor of more than a hundred Apple *patents*.

"Apple's DNA has always been to try to *democratize* technology," Steve said. He's said he believed that if Apple made something "really great, then everybody [would] want to use it."

Steve reflected on the many turns his life had taken when he spoke to the graduates at Stanford University. And he used his experiences as life lessons for the young people in the audience, so they could benefit from the very valuable lessons he had learned.

I'm pretty sure none of this would have happened if I hadn't been fired from Apple. It was awful-tasting medicine, but I guess the patient needed it. Sometimes life hits you in the head with a brick. Don't lose faith. I'm convinced that the only thing that kept me going was that I loved what I did. You've got to find what you love. Your work is going to fill a large part of your life, and the only way to be truly satisfied is to do what you believe is great work. And the only way to do great work is to love what you do. If you haven't found it yet, keep looking. Don't settle. As with all matters of the heart, you'll know when you find it. And, like any great relationship, it just gets better and better as the years roll on. So keep looking until you find it. Don't settle.

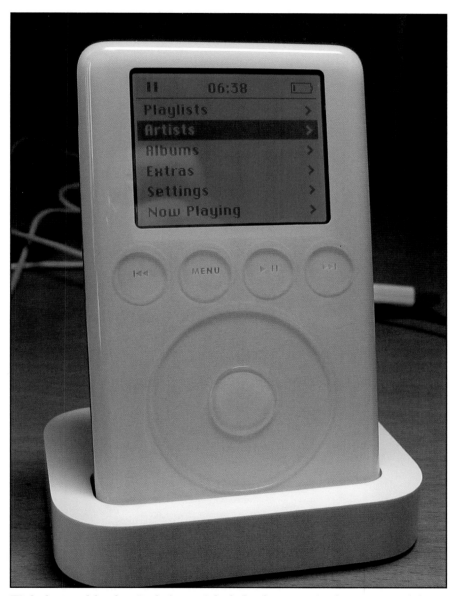

With devices like the iPod, Steve Jobs helped to turn Apple into one of the most successful technology companies of all time. And all after coming back to the company after being fired!

CHAPTER 3
APPLE ON TOP

Words to Know

MP3 player: An MP3 player is a device that can play MP3s, computer files that contain sound, like music, an audio book, or a recording of a lecture. Most MP3 players are portable and are used with headphones.

With Steve back at the top of the company, Apple was poised to become one of the most talked-about and beloved companies in the world. In 1998, the company introduced the iMac, a new Macintosh computer with a colorful design. The iMac was a huge hit, and paved the way for Apple's move toward being known for easy-to-use, good-looking technology. One new creation, however, would become one of Apple's signature products, bringing the company a whole new level of success.

Apple Creates the iPod

In 2001, Apple unveiled the iPod, a digital music player. With Apple's iPod, owners could take the music they had stored on their computer and then transfer it to their iPod, so they could listen anywhere. The iPod wasn't the first of its kind, but the device looked good and was easy to use.

The iPod marked a shift in the music industry and at Apple. By the end of the 1990s, more and more people were listening to music on computers, rather than off of CDs. With an **MP3 player**, you could carry around hundreds of CDs worth of music in your pocket. You could store more than that on a computer. With a CD player, you had to listen to one CD at a time, but with digital music, you could listen to any song in your collection whenever you wanted. The iPod was part of the movement toward digital music taking over the industry.

The device was also part of Apple moving away from only creating computers. With the iPod, Apple was shifting its strategy slightly. Apple saw an opening in the MP3 player market, and it created the best product it could. The company would do the same thing with later products as well. It focused on a section of technology that was becoming increasingly popular, and then created a high-quality version of that idea.

When the iPod first went on sale in November of 2001, Apple's newest product sold well. Just a few years later, however, the iPod became a major hit, selling millions of units. By 2005, the iPod was selling several million units per year. It was one of the most popular MP3 players available. Soon, iPods seemed to be everywhere, on television and named in music, on buses and trains, in schools and offices. For many people, the iPod became the main way to listen to music.

In 2003, Apple began selling digital music in their iTunes Store. The iPod was based around a change in the music industry from CDs to digital, and the iTunes Store was the next step in that direction. The service sold songs for $0.99 each, rather than as an album. Instead of having to buy a whole CD for the one song that you liked, you could just buy that one song.

Over the next few years, digital music would become bigger and bigger, with digital music selling as much, and sometimes more, than CDs. The iTunes Store became the biggest outlet for digital music online, with more sales going through iTunes than any other service. By 2010, the iTunes Store had sold ten billion songs.

Once the original iPod was released, Apple began perfecting their newest device. The company put out many different versions of their MP3 player, changing key things about the iPod such as the controls and its size. Eventually, Apple released an iPod with touch-screen controls called the iPod Touch.

The iPhone Takes Over

In the same way the iPod was perfect for the time in which it was created and released, the iPhone, Apple's next big idea, was the right device at the right time. In the time after the iPod's release, the cell phone industry moved toward what are called smart phones, phones that can do more than make calls. Many smart phones can play music, watch video, surf the Internet, and more. As it became clear that smart phones were the future, Apple again saw an opportunity to enter a new section of the technology industry. They set about creating a new smart phone built to be simple, and they took advantage of the growing demand for phones that functioned like computers.

Apple fans wait outside an AT&T store for the release of the iPhone in 2007.

Steve Jobs showed the world the iPhone in January of 2007. The phone was entirely controlled through its touch screen. It also had a built-in camera and speakers. With the device, you could make calls and send text messages, take pictures and listen to music, surf the Internet, and watch YouTube. In addition, iPhone owners could download programs called "apps," short for applications, from the iTunes App Store. Apps could be anything from a game to a program that gave new uses to the phone. You might download a cookbook app to learn how to make a new dish. You might download an app that allowed you to talk to your friends on Facebook. With the inclusion of apps, the iPhone seemed like it could do anything, and be anything, the owner wanted.

When the iPhone was finally released in the summer of 2007, excitement was running high. Apple fans couldn't wait to get the next creation from the company that had brought them the iPod. On the night of the iPhone's release, people lined up at AT&T and Apple stores around the United States, all hoping to take home one of Steve Jobs' latest gadgets.

The iPhone was another success for Apple, selling more than 140,000 units in just a few days. Over the next few months, the phone would sell more and more, becoming increasingly popular. Just as the iPod had worked its way into pop culture, so too did the iPhone find its way onto television and into hit songs. The iPhone was the cool device to have because it was from Apple. For many, any new device from Apple is reason to be excited.

Just as was the case with the iPod, as soon as the iPhone was released, Apple began working on the next version of the device.

With the next iPhones, the 3G and 3GS, Apple was able to make their phone work faster, particularly on the Internet. After that, the iPhone 4 changed the look of Apple's phone slightly, and brought new features like FaceTime, a way to talk to other iPhone owners using video.

Apple's Next Big Thing: The iPad

In January 2010, Steve announced that Apple would begin selling the iPad, the company's first tablet computer, in April. The device had a touch screen, just like the iPhone and the newest version of the iPod. It could go online, download apps, and check e-mail, just like the iPhone. But the iPad's screen was much larger than the iPhone, making it better for watching videos or reading digital books. Apple announced that they'd be selling digital books through iBooks, a section of the iTunes Store, exclusively on the iPad.

In the three months that the iPad was first available for purchase, Apple sold more than three million units. The iPad became a giant success almost as soon as it launched. Though tablet computers had been around before, the iPad introduced many more people to the idea of holding a computer in their hands. Few other tablets were as easy for people to pick up and use. The iPad was even popular with people who'd never learned to use a computer. These people found that the touch screen of the iPad and large, bright screen was easier for them to use than a regular mouse and keyboard. Schools and universities saw that the iPad could work well in the classroom, and began experimenting with ways of bringing the iPad into learning.

Today, the iPad is the most popular kind of tablet computer. Apple has sold millions of its latest device around the world.

Steve Jobs and Microsoft founder Bill Gates discuss the future of technology in 2007.

Though it wasn't the first tablet computer, for many people it is the only tablet with which they're familiar. The iPad, like the iPhone and iPod before it, has become the leader in a new, increasingly popular segment of the technology industry.

It seems no matter what Apple puts out, people want it immediately. Apple products are sleek, well designed, and easy to use. The company's products solve the problems other devices can't seem to, and as a result, they sell far better than almost all their competition. And in charge of it all was Steve Jobs, the man behind Apple's success.

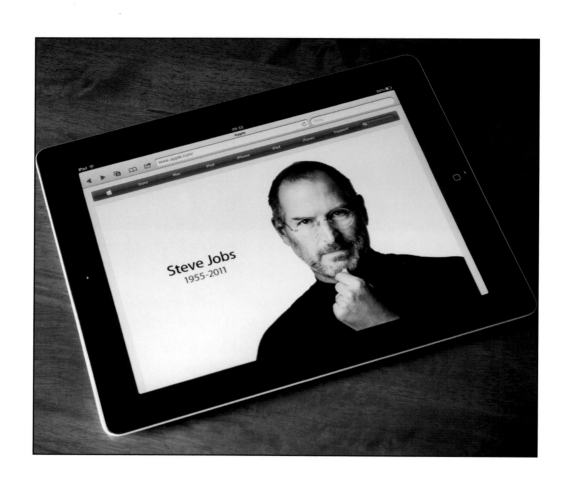

CHAPTER 4
REMEMBERING STEVE JOBS TODAY

Words to Know

dogma: Dogma are principles laid down by authority figures as being absolutely true.

iconic: If something is iconic, it is a symbol known to many people.

In 2003, Steve's life was once again put into perspective after a frightening brush with death. Steve, a Buddhist and a vegetarian, always took care of his health—but when he went to the doctor one morning, a scan showed a tumor on his pancreas. His doctors told him it was most likely a type of cancer that could not be cured, and he likely only had three to six months to live.

"I didn't even know what a pancreas was," Steve said later.

My doctor advised me to go home and get my affairs in order, which is doctor's code for prepare to die. It means to try to tell your kids everything you thought you'd have the next ten years to tell them in just a few months. It means to make sure everything is buttoned up so that it will be as easy as possible for your family. It means to say your goodbyes.

Health Concerns

After spending the day coping with the prospect of his own death, and thinking about his life, Jobs went for a biopsy. With his wife by his side, doctors took a sample of the cells from the tumor.

"I was sedated, but my wife, who was there, told me that when they viewed the cells under a microscope the doctors started crying because it turned out to be a very rare form of pancreatic cancer that is curable with surgery," Steve said later.

Steve had surgery at Stanford University Medical Center in Palo Alto, near his home, and he was given a clean bill of health. "No one wants to die," Steve said.

Even people who want to go to heaven don't want to die to get there. And yet death is the destination we all share. No one has ever escaped it. And that is as it should be, because Death is very likely the single best invention of Life. It is Life's change agent. It clears out the old to make way for the new.

"When I was seventeen, I read a quote that went something like, 'If you live each day as if it was your last, someday you'll most certainly be right.'" Steve said.

It made an impression on me, and since then, for the past thirty-three years, I have looked in the mirror every morning

Jobs worked for Apple as long as he could before leaving the company due to his health problems.

and asked myself, "If today were the last day of my life, would I want to do what I am about to do today?" And whenever the answer has been "No" for too many days in a row, I know I need to change something.

Living with cancer for so many years, as well his public firing and humble beginnings, helped Steve see his life clearly. He valued each and every moment of it for the opportunities it held, as he told the Stanford students in 2005.

Remembering that I'll be dead soon is the most important tool I've ever encountered to help me make the big choices in life. Because almost everything—all external expectations, all pride, all fear of embarrassment or failure—these things just fall away in the face of death, leaving only what is truly important. Remembering that you are going to die is the best way I know to avoid the trap of thinking you have something to lose. You are already naked. There is no reason not to follow your heart.

Jobs took every opportunity he could to share that message with the people of the world he helped change. His lasting legacy—more than iPods, Mac Books, *Toy Story*, or any of his other contributions—is the example he set of what people can do when they work hard to make their dreams come true and believe in themselves.

Steve Jobs' introduction of new Apple devices became legendary among technology fans.

"Your time is limited, so don't waste it living someone else's life," Steve told the 2005 graduating class of Stanford University.

Don't be trapped by *dogma*—which is living with the results of other people's thinking. Don't let the noise of others' opinions drown out your own inner voice. And most important, have the courage to follow your heart and intuition. They somehow already know what you truly want to become. Everything else is secondary.

Steve's Death

Steve battled cancer for years, all while working to make Apple the most successful technology company in the world. In the time since his diagnosis, Jobs shared the iPhone and iPad with the world. Not even cancer could stop Jobs from giving the world more amazing new products that would change communication forever.

In August, 2011, Steve decided he couldn't keep working as CEO of Apple and fight his cancer at the same time. He told Apple fans and customers he would be stepping down from the position he'd held two different times.

"I have always said that if there ever came a day when I could no longer meet my duties and expectations as Apple's CEO, I would be the first to let you know," Jobs wrote in a letter put out by Apple. "Unfortunately, that day has come."

Though Steve survived for many years longer than the three to six months doctors first gave him, Steve passed away in October of 2011. He'd lived for almost ten years since being diagnosed with cancer. Steve was just 56 years old when he died of complications from his pancreatic cancer.

Steve's sister Mona described his last moments. When she arrived at his Palo Alto home, she said, "[Steve] and his wife, Laurene, were talking and joking, and the kids were gathered around him." Soon after, Mona said that, just before he died, Steve looked off into the distance and said "Oh WOW! Oh WOW! Oh WOW!" Steve's final words seem to perfectly suit the way he lived his life, always searching for the beautiful, surprising, wondrous aspects of life.

Famous business and world leaders from around the globe were touched by Steve's death. The President of the United States spoke of Steve Jobs' life and legacy. Few people are as loved all around the world as Steve Jobs was.

Bill Gates, the founder of Apple's rival, Microsoft, wrote this about working with Steve: "For those of us lucky enough to get to work with Steve, it's been an insanely great honor. I will miss Steve immensely."

Around the world, people considered how Apple's founder had changed their lives. Steve had given the world so much, and now he was gone. Many reacted as if they'd known him personally. For so many Apple fans, Steve was more than the CEO of a great company. He was a visionary and a leader. He was someone people looked up to. It was as if Steve had stepped into the future and brought back the best of what was to come each time he pulled another sleek Apple device from his pocket. "There is one

Apple fans and admirers of Jobs' work left a memorial in New York City for the technology pioneer after his death.

Apple devices like the iPad have changed the way people use the Internet, read books, listen to music, watch movies, and talk to their loved ones.

more thing. . . . ," Steve always said. Now Apple fans knew there would be no "one more thing" from Jobs. The world had lost one of its brightest minds.

Still, though the world was saddened at the news of Jobs' death, his vision for a connected future lives on, as do the products he helped to bring us.

Remembering Steve Jobs Today

The lives of just about everyone in America—and millions of people around the world—have been touched in some way by the creative endeavors of Steve Jobs. Whether it's someone listening to an iPod on their way to school, people using Apple computers to do their jobs, or families watching the latest exciting Pixar release, the impact that Steve has had on modern culture is undeniable. Few people have done as much to shape the course of technology in the twenty-first century. With their Macintosh, iPod, iPhone, and iPad, Apple is in a class of its own when it comes to technology companies. With millions of devices sold, Apple's is a success story like few others.

Before his death, Steve was one of America's most well-known billionaires, worth more than six billion dollars in 2010. He was been named one of *Forbes* magazine's World's Most Powerful People, *Fortune Magazine*'s CEO of the decade, and person of the year by *Time* magazine and the *Financial Times*.

Steve's presence at an Apple event was unmistakable. His glasses, jeans, and black shirts, have all became *iconic* for millions around the world who watched each event patiently to see if

Walter Issacson, who's also written biographies of famous inventors Benjamin Franklin and Albert Einstein, was writing Steve Jobs' biography when he died. The book, published after Jobs died, was a massive success around the world in many different languages.

Steve would pull a new Apple device from his pocket or announce the next million-selling gadget. For many, the excitement of a new Apple product is enough to make them buy it on the first day it's available. With Steve Jobs gone, many wonder whether Apple will be able to continue to innovate and succeed in the same ways the company did under the former-CEO and co-founder.

At the time of his death, Steve had become one of one of the biggest names in the technology industry, as well as one of the most famous businessmen in the world. Steve helped Apple, the company he helped start, become a massive success, introducing products that are easy to use and sell well. Few people ever achieve the kinds of success that Steve Jobs did in his life.

And he did it all without a college degree!

WHAT CAN YOU EXPECT?

Of course not everyone who skips college is going to be a celebrity or a millionaire. But there are other more ordinary jobs out there for people who choose to go a different route from college. Here's what you can expect to make in 100 of the top-paying jobs available to someone who has only a high school diploma. (If you're not sure what any of the jobs are, look them up on the Internet to find out more about them.) Keep in mind that these are average salaries; a beginning worker will likely make much less, while someone with many more years of experience could make much more. Also, remember that wages for the same jobs vary somewhat in different parts of the country.

Position	Average Annual Salary
rotary drill operators (oil & gas)	$59,560
commercial divers	$58,060
railroad conductors & yardmasters	$54,900
chemical plant & system operators	$54,010
real estate sales agents	$53,100
subway & streetcar operators	$52,800
postal service clerks	$51,670
pile-driver operators	$51,410
railroad brake, signal & switch operators	$49,600

brickmasons & blockmasons	$49,250
postal service mail carriers	$48,940
gaming supervisors	$48,920
postal service mail sorters & processors	$48,260
gas compressor & gas pumping station operators	$47,860
roof bolters (mining)	$47,750
forest fire fighters	$47,270
private detectives & investigators	$47,130
tapers	$46,880
continuous mining machine operators	$46,680
rail car repairers	$46,430
shuttle car operators	$46,400
rail-track laying & maintenance equipment operators	$46,000
chemical equipment operators & tenders	$45,100
explosives workers (ordnance handling experts & blasters)	$45,030
makeup artists (theatrical & performance)	$45,010
sheet metal workers	$44,890
managers/supervisors of landscaping & groundskeeping workers	$44,080
loading machine operators (underground mining)	$43,970
rough carpenters	$43,640

derrick operators (oil & gas)	$43,590
flight attendants	$43,350
refractory materials repairers (except brickmasons)	$43,310
production, planning & expediting clerks	$43,260
mine cutting & channeling machine operators	$43,120
fabric & apparel patternmakers	$42,940
service unit operators (oil, gas, & mining)	$42,690
tile & marble setters	$42,450
paperhangers	$42,310
bridge & lock tenders	$41,630
hoist & winch operators	$41,620
carpet installers	$41,560
pump operators (except wellhead pumpers)	$41,490
terrazzo workers & finishers	$41,360
plasterers & stucco masons	$41,260
painters (transportation equipment)	$41,220
automotive body & related repairers	$41,020
hazardous materials removal workers	$40,270
bailiffs	$40,240
wellhead pumpers	$40,210
maintenance workers (machinery)	$39,570
truck drivers (heavy & tractor-trailer)	$39,260

floor layers (except carpet, wood & hard tiles)	$39,190
managers of retail sales workers	$39,130
cargo & freight agents	$38,940
metal-refining furnace operators & tenders	$38,830
excavating & loading machine and dragline operators	$38,540
separating, filtering, clarifying & still machine operators	$38,450
motorboat operators	$38,390
dredge operators	$38,330
lay-out workers (metal & plastic)	$38,240
forest fire inspectors & prevention specialists	$38,180
medical & clinical laboratory technicians	$37,860
tire builders	$37,830
dental laboratory technicians	$37,690
paving, surfacing & tamping equipment operators	$37,660
locksmiths & safe repairers	$37,550
sailors & marine oilers	$37,310
dispatchers (except police, fire & ambulance)	$37,310
pipelayers	$37,040
helpers (extraction workers)	$36,870

rolling machine setters, operators & tenders	$36,670
welders, cutters & welder fitters	$36,630
solderers & brazers	$36,630
gem & diamond workers	$36,620
police, fire & ambulance dispatchers	$36,470
models	$36,420
meter readers (utilities)	$36,400
mechanical door repairers	$36,270
public address system & other announcers	$36,130
rail yard engineers, dinkey operators & hostlers	$36,090
bus drivers (transit & intercity)	$35,990
insurance policy processing clerks	$35,740
insurance claims clerks	$35,740
computer-controlled machine tool operators (metal and plastic)	$35,570
license clerks	$35,570
court clerks	$35,570
fallers	$35,570
septic tank servicers & sewer pipe cleaners	$35,470
parking enforcement workers	$35,360
highway maintenance workers	$35,310
floor sanders & finishers	$35,140

tool grinders, filers, & sharpeners	$35,110
paper goods machine setters, operators & tenders	$35,040
printing machine operators	$35,030
inspectors, testers, sorters, samplers & weighers	$34,840
pourers & casters (metal)	$34,760
loan interviewers & clerks	$34,670
furnace, kiln, oven, drier & kettle operators & tenders	$34,410
recreational vehicle service technicians	$34,320
roustabouts (oil & gas)	$34,190

Source: Bureau of Labor Statistics, U.S. Department of Labor, 2008.

Find Out More

In Books

Cooke, C. W. *Steve Jobs: Cofounder of Apple.* Beverly Hills, Calif.: Bluewater, 2011.

Isaacson, Walter. Steve Jobs. New York: Simon & Schuster, 2012.

Kahney, Leander. *Inside Steve's Brain.* Portland, Ore: Portfolio, 2009.

Moritz, Michael. *Return to the Little Kingdom: Steve Jobs and the Creation of Apple.* New York: Overlook Press, 2010.

Young, Jeffrey S. and William L. Simon. *icon Steve Jobs: The Greatest Second Act In the History Business.* Hoboken, N.J.: John Wiley and Sons, 2005.

On the Internet

Forbes Magazine: Steve Jobs' Profile
www.forbes.com/profile/steve-jobs

Stanford University News: Text of Steve Jobs' Commencement Address (2005)
news.stanford.edu/news/2005/june15/jobs-061505.html

TED.com: Steve Jobs: How to Live Before You Die
www.ted.com/talks/steve_jobs_how_to_live_before_you_die.html

Index

Picture Credits

Al Luckow: p. 25
Cacophony: p. 16
Coolcaesar: p. 15
Danamania: p. 26
Glenn Fleishman: p. 52
Joe Ravi: p. 12
Joi Ito: p. 43
ken.gz: p. 47, 48
Łukasz Ryba: p. 35
Malpass93: p. 33
Matt Buchanan: p. 11
Matthew Yohe: p. 8
Mircea Nicolescu | Dreamstime.com: p. 51
mylerdude: p. 22
Nadiaa Gerbish | Dreamstime.com: p. 54
Padraic Ryan: p. 40
Yangrill | Dreamstime.com: p. 19

About the Author

Jaime A. Seba studied political science at Syracuse University before switching her focus to communications. She has worked both in New York and on the West Coast as an activist for LGBT awareness. She is currently a freelance writer based in Seattle.